Praise for Say It Simply: 8 Easy Steps to Turn Readers into Clients

"Move beyond *I don't know how* and break through inertia. Be invited to breathe freely as you express. Follow Nina's steps, and witness ideas transform into gems that flow from your heart through your hands and onto the page with ease."

Janet M. Harvey
ICF Certified Master Certified Coach
CEO inviteCHANGE

"As I read *Say It Simply*, I felt like Nina sat by my side as my coach, and it validated my own experience of writing a book. I wish I had read this book before I started writing mine. It would have been a far simpler process and an easier experience. Nina is doing a great service for her clients by showing them the path before they walk it. Her leadership will guide others by encouraging them to step out of their comfort zone and write down their words for their legacy."

Elisa Hawkinson
Author of *Calming Your Chaos*

"In your hands you hold a practical and proven blueprint for writing the right book and growing your business or career. You will set yourself apart from your competition and position your expertise in a whole new and exciting way."

Mark LeBlanc
Author of *Growing Your Business* and *Never Be the Same*
Chairman, Indie Books International

"While *Say It Simply* aims to help you write a book that's a client-attraction magnet, it does much more than that. It provides a framework with which to think about every business communication you create. Durfee coaches you through the process with an encouraging tone, practical advice, and personal stories of success and failure. Simply said: "Writing a book? Get this book!"

Beth L. Buelow, PCC
Author of *The Introvert Entrepreneur:
Amplify Your Strength and Create Success on Your Own
Terms*

Praise for Full Bloom: 7 Practical Steps to Get What You Want +1 to Grow On

"Divinely inspired. Awesome. Lovely, gorgeous. Simple, soul-full."

Fran Fisher, MCC
Author of *Violet's Vision*

"Nina Durfee is the quintessential manifestor, and in her book, *Full Bloom: 7 Practical Steps to Get What You Want + 1 to Grow On,* she describes her walk with the process of mastering intentional change. She has distilled the key elements from her own journey to identify these beautifully simple 7+1 steps that lead directly to success, no matter what your goal. Her chapter exercises provide an immediate "how to," making it effortless to step from "being," to "thinking," to "doing!" If you are feeling stuck, currently out of touch with your life, or just looking to create your own next chapter, I highly recommend this delightful read *for you!*

Anna Goldsworthy
the Possibility Detective
Author of *Feel Good No Matter What*

Say It Simply

8 Easy Steps to **Turn Readers** into **Clients**

NINA DURFEE

BALBOA.
PRESS

A DIVISION OF HAY HOUSE

Balboa Press books may be ordered through booksellers or by contacting:

Balboa Press
A Division of Hay House
1663 Liberty Drive
Bloomington, IN 47403
www.balboapress.com
1 (877) 407-4847

Because of the dynamic nature of the Internet, any web addresses or links contained in this book may have changed since publication and may no longer be valid. The views expressed in this work are solely those of the author and do not necessarily reflect the views of the publisher, and the publisher hereby disclaims any responsibility for them.

The author of this book does not dispense medical advice or prescribe the use of any technique as a form of treatment for physical, emotional, or medical problems without the advice of a physician, either directly or indirectly. The intent of the author is only to offer information of a general nature to help you in your quest for emotional and spiritual well-being. In the event you use any of the information in this book for yourself, which is your constitutional right, the author and the publisher assume no responsibility for your actions.

This book is a work of non-fiction. Unless otherwise noted, the author and the publisher make no explicit guarantees as to the accuracy of the information contained in this book and in some cases, names of people and places have been altered to protect their privacy.

Any people depicted in stock imagery provided by Getty Images are models, and such images are being used for illustrative purposes only.

Certain stock imagery © Getty Images.

Print information available on the last page.

ISBN: 978-1-5043-9749-0 (sc)
ISBN: 978-1-5043-9750-6 (e)

Balboa Press rev. date: 03/14/2018

To independent business owners
who want to showcase your genius
by speaking your truth from your heart
to resonate with your ideal client.

ACKNOWLEDGMENTS

I deeply appreciate the cadre of mentors, authors, publishers, philosophers, and other wise souls, alive and long passed, for your education, critique, inspiration, and guidance. Especially, I thank Anna Goldsworthy for our business partnership, for our deep friendship, and for igniting the world and my life with color, laughter, and joy; Cyndi Dady for your generosity, encouragement, and the softness you add to the world; Rebecca West, for your innate creativity, clarity, and generosity; Caron MacLane for encouraging my first step on a new journey; David for your unconditional love, your eternal good humor, and your blind faith in me; and my Tulip Petals (you know who you are) for holding my hand on the ever unfolding and surprising path of self-discovery.

TABLE OF CONTENTS

INTRODUCTION

Do you want business growth to be easier and less stressful? Would you enjoy smoother conversion from prospect to client? What if you had a tool that demonstrates your expertise, enhances your visibility, sets you apart from others in your field, evokes invitations to speak, and reduces the pressure of marketing?

That tool is your Signature Book.

Your Signature Book is your imprint on humanity. Your Signature Book will:

- Elevate your feeling of personal accomplishment and satisfaction
- Enhance your confidence in your product, your service, and your Self
- Anchor your credibility as an expert
- Turn prospects to clients
- Establish your wisdom, your philosophy, and your legacy

To accomplish that requires a handful of essential elements, the "Easy Steps" that I will outline in the chapters ahead. The foundational element is a *main point* or overarching principle that is clear, concise, and compelling.

The power of language is not so much in what we say as in how we say it.

Eric T. Wagner, Founder and CEO of Mighty Wise Academy: A Virtual Academy for Entrepreneurship and contributing advisor for www.Forbes.com, says, "failure to communicate value propositions in clear, concise and compelling fashion" is one of the top five reasons 8 out of 10 entrepreneurs who start a business fail within 18 months.

My purpose with this book is to improve the odds for solopreneurs.

Aside from delivering a quality product or service, two key elements for entrepreneurial success are visibility and credibility. No matter how good you are at what you do, no matter how much you know, no matter how much better your widget is than all the other widgets, if people don't see you, they can't buy from you. But visibility isn't enough. Assuming you are seen, what makes you stand out from the rest of the crowd as the go-to expert in your field?

This is the crux of marketing: to attract attention and create interest for the purpose of selling a product or service. Small business owners (and big business owners, for that matter) attempt this in a multitude of ways: elevator pitches, leveraging the community, collaborating, networking, asking for referrals, building relationships, offering coupons. Problem is, everyone else is doing that too—which means no one stands out as unique.

Jack Canfield, author of The Success Principles and creator of the best-selling Chicken Soup for the Soul series, says that being published increases your visibility and credibility.

How does having a Signature Book make business easier? Look at it from the standpoint of the business prospect. Imagine that you are in the market for the services of a professional organizer. You walk into a networking event, filled with entrepreneurs, two of whom are professional organizers. Each has a business card, a website, and some expertise about organizing personal and business space. One of them has published a book on how to calm your chaos by organizing your space, detailing the ins and outs of organizing, offering tools, processes, and examples. She holds the book in her hand.

Which person are you inclined to approach?

In a network setting, a book in the hand invites easy conversation. It takes the pressure off clumsy introductions and settles the jitters about what to say. As a common focus, it establishes an immediate and natural bond of attention.

Next, you discover that both organizers offer workshops. You are ripe for that kind of learning environment and eager to attend.

Whose workshop will you choose?

The book offers instant credibility, conveying an image of orderly thinking, expertise, and educational prowess. After all, in order to write a book on the topic, the author must know her stuff—right? Your Signature Book graciously opens the door to potential clients and invites them to easily engage with you. Simple, classy hospitality.

That's great for writers, you say, but what about us "nonwriters"?

For that I have two responses:

First: *baloney.* Everything you do centers around communication, and you write every day. You send e-mails, you text, you write an ad, you make a list, you design a process, you make a flyer, you host a blog, you take copious notes. You do all this so that you can convey a message, tell a story, elicit a response, produce a result.

Second: Even if you consider yourself a nonwriter, you are an expert in your field. You are graced with characteristics that make you unique. You have your own style of speaking, behaving, believing, and engaging with others. Your business purpose, your mission, and your vision are based on core values specific to you.

To create the book that is your signature business tool, you need only a formula and a competent editor. *Say It Simply* outlines the formula consisting of 8 Easy Steps to evoke reader response.

Whether you write a how-to manual or a self-help book, whether you describe a product or a service, whether you offer a diagnostic tool or a where-to-go-from-here map, your Signature Book showcases your genius and tells your story your way. The tone and content of your book will reveal your passion, your expertise, and your wisdom so that readers will know right away that *this speaks to me and I want some!*

In the chapters ahead, you will learn how to zero in on your main point and convey it in a way that is clear, concise, and compelling. You'll learn the importance of packaging your product in powerful prose. I'm not talking about the great American novel here. David Ogilvy, late founder of Ogilvy & Mather (advertising), said you must open with gusto:

When I write an advertisement, I don't want you
to tell me that you find it "creative." I want you to
find it so interesting that you buy the product.

That's what it is to be compelling, and this book will
tell you why that is so important and what happens if
you fall short. You'll understand the ramifications of not
sifting out the chaff to reveal the kernel, the very core
of your message. You will see the value of offering your
client a vision of possibility, and you will envision your
own fantastic success. You will learn valuable tips and
engage in practical exercises, and you will be inspired
to create similar tools for your readers. You will learn
how to use the voice of your heart to rivet your readers
with pertinent stories. You will learn how offering your
own challenges and failures elicits the empathy and trust
of your readers and potential clients. You will learn to
simplify your call to action so that your ideal clients will
have an easy avenue to engage with you. You will learn
the impact of speaking less and saying more.

Finally, you will discover the step that separates
the amateurs from the professionals in the world of
publication.

Your Signature Book is a powerful testament to
your expertise. *Say It Simply* offers a proven formula to
write YOUR signature book. Your success lies in the
expression of your wisdom using the 8 Easy Steps set

forth in the pages that follow. Employ these 8 Easy Steps to create material that is clear, concise, and compelling.

Showcase your genius.

Change ho-hum to zowie.

Wow your clients.

Succeed beyond what you dare to hope!

Get published. Be noticed.

EASY STEP #1
What

Make Your Main Point
Clear, Concise, and Compelling

Omit needless words.
Strunk & White

Your *main point* is the core message you want your reader to know. It's the overarching premise that will serve your reader, and it is the platform from which the rest of your material is launched.

Anything you write—a book, a chapter, a paragraph, an article, a blog, a marketing flier, an e-mail, a web page—has a *main point*. The *main point* must be clear enough to let the reader know her level of interest. It helps her decide whether or not to read on.

State your *main point* clearly and succinctly. Here's why:

According to the Statistic Brain Research Institute[1] the average attention span in 2015 is 8.25 seconds. That's down from an average of 12 seconds in 2000. An average web page contains 593 words, and you can expect a reader to read no more than 28% of those words. When the number of words is reduced to 111, the reader will pick up 49%. That means you must grip the interest of the reader in your opening comment. The more words it takes, the less powerful your grip. When your grip slips, she walks away, your message goes unheard, and you lose her as a prospect.

Not only does concise expression work to your advantage, but brevity and clarity also respect the reader's time, attention, and intellect. Content that is clear, concise, and compelling eliminates reader fatigue. In fact, it energizes your reader to read on and learn more. The more of your content the readers read, the more likely they are to follow up and do business with you. Clear, concise, compelling content leads to more clients, more income, and more happiness for you.

On your web page, honor the reader with crisp, clean bullet points. If you can't resist the temptation to expound, offer a link to the exposition on another page, but don't burden the reader at first contact.

---

[1] http://www.statisticbrain.com/attention-span-statistics/ quoting the source: Harald Weinreich, Hartmut Obendorf, Eelco Herder, and Matthias Mayer: "Not Quite the Average: An Empirical Study of Web Use," in the ACM Transactions on the Web, vol. 2, no. 1 (February 2008), article #5.

For a book, you may convey the *main point* in a chapter title or subsection heading, but don't expect the title or heading to carry the weight. Restate or reframe your *main point* in the opening sentence of that segment or chapter. Restatement acts to support and retain readers like me who tend to skip over titles and subheads to get to the meat of the matter.

WORK IT

Craft your *main point*

A prerequisite to expressing a clear *main point* to the reader is author understanding. Use this prompt to zero in on your *main point*:

What is your overarching premise? The overarching premise is the grand master that drives the subsequent content. Every point that follows must serve the overarching premise or suffer a grave demise. (The *main point* for this book is that your *main point* must be clear, concise, and compelling.)

Write a rough version of your *main point* here:

_____

_____

How does the main point serve your reader?

If the *main point* doesn't serve your reader, you are wasting your energy. The reader is there to be served, and it's up to you to offer that service. Know your service and know how it benefits the reader. (This chapter, for example, explains in detail how my *main point* serves you.)

What ideas support your main point?

A variety of key points support your big-picture message. Brainstorm on paper as many supporting points as you can. Don't hold back. Toss in anything remotely related and useful. The value of this process is twofold. First, a list of supporting elements can serve as a rough outline of what is to follow in your book. It's a trigger that generates content. Second, the juicy mix of ideas may reveal a truer version of your *main point*. In the space below, list every idea, big and small, significant and insignificant, complex and simple, serious and silly, that feels important. Include on the list the overarching point you expressed above.

List your main ideas here:

Put a checkmark by the top 10 most important points. Some of these ideas may serve as chapter headings or subheadings.

From those 10, circle your top three favorites.

Which of the three is most critical? **This is your main point.** Aim to express it in fewer than 10 words. Express it fully in one sentence here:

_____

_____

Less is more

Resist the urge to overexplain. Compare this statement:

> Don't bombard your reader with an excessive amount of verbiage, even if the words make you sound sophisticated and knowledgeable.

with this statement:

> Say it simply.

Which expression packs more punch?

Benefits for the reader

A clear *main point* benefits the reader because:

1. It is unambiguous. It addresses one thing only.
2. It is simply stated and easily understood, leaving no room for misinterpretation.
3. It is relevant. The overarching *main point* forms the foundation for everything that follows.
4. It honors the reader's time and eliminates reader fatigue.
5. It anchors the learning that follows.

Benefits for you

A clear *main point* is a touchstone for you as the writer. When your writing takes a tangent and you struggle for cohesiveness, the *main point* is your compass. Eliminate anything that doesn't serve it, and you are right back on track.

A clear *main point* facilitates reader understanding. If your reader misinterprets your message, you defeat your purpose before you can gain any traction. A muddy message begs the reader to toss your book in a corner and go binge on chocolate. The poor reader who tries to stick it out is saddled with wading through your material, struggling to understand, and wasting time. His efforts will leave him feeling inept, frustrated, disgruntled, betrayed, and even angry. No matter how nice you are or how expert in your field, an angry reader can sully your reputation in no time flat. Not only have you sent him screaming into the street never to do business with you again, but you've erected a barrier to potential future clients by sabotaging your credibility.

A clear *main point* puts your reader at ease. Clarity engenders trust, conserves time and energy, and engages the reader to learn more. Even if he decides your message is not for him, he has made an informed choice. He's done so from a place of trust and certainty and without feeling betrayed. Whether he stays in or opts out, he holds a positive impression of you and your business. When he finds others who seek what you offer, he can confidently point them in your direction. Your solid reputation remains intact.

The main point of each segment or chapter should serve your overarching *main point*.

WORK IT

Put it to use

- Practice expressing your *main point* in four different ways:
    1. As an e-mail subject line
    2. As a book or article title
    3. As the opening line for a book
    4. As a web page header

- Get feedback. Show samples to friends, clients, or colleagues. Ask them to interpret the meaning.
- Revise as desired.

Congratulations! You've crafted a clear *main point.* Now all you have to do is defend it. I'll show you how with Easy Step #2.

EASY STEP #2
Why

Explain the Importance
of Your Main Point

It's not what you do, it's why you do it that makes a difference.
Jennifer Louden

The *why* of your main point is the hook that keeps us reading. Now that you've articulated your *main point* clearly, tell me *why* I should care. Whether your *main point* is verifiable (the longitude/latitude of the Great Pyramid of Giza), a hypothesis (all daisies have the same number of petals), or a belief (candidate A is better than candidate B), if I don't know *why* it's important, I won't stick around.

In support of my *main point* that content should be clear, concise, and compelling, I offer the wisdom of Eric T. Wagner, Founder of Mighty Wise Academy for Entrepreneurship and contributing advisor for www. Forbes.com. Eric tells us that "failure to communicate value propositions in clear, concise and compelling fashion" is one of the top five reasons 8 out of 10 entrepreneurs who start a business fail within 18 months.

The feeling of failure is the feeling of loss. Failure in business is about loss of valuable time and effort, loss of money, loss of respect, and loss of confidence. Our ultimate reason for wanting anything, including a successful business, is that we are sure we will feel better when we have it. Even when we feel good, we're always looking to feel better. We want more time, more money, more freedom, more ease. Content that makes your reader feel hopeful about your service or product serves a valuable function. It catalyzes her into inspired, optimistic action to realize her desire to feel good.

If your goal is to bring in more clients and more money, the statistic offered by Eric T. Wagner is meaty support for crafting a clear, concise, and compelling *main point*. And without a compelling *why*, your reader will abandon your message like yesterday's underwear.

To help carve out your *why*, start by naming three life areas that might be affected if your *main point* is ignored. Include a big-picture reason and a close-up reason. Know why your message is important from your own measure of core values, life experience, and desired outcome. From there, extrapolate the impact on your reader. Support your *why* with both logical and emotional evidence.

Trigger the worry, frustration, or dissatisfaction that will result if your *main point* is ignored.

To touch on logic and emotion, offer a statistic, an example, a quote, or a story to show how the *main point* affects the reader's experience. For best results, demonstrate the effect on at least one of these five life areas: health, wealth, relationship, sex, identity. I call these the Big 5 Concerns.

Examples (with Big 5 Concern in parentheses)

Main Point: "Carrots are essential for good health" (health). Tie it to the reader's experience by informing her, for example, that eating carrots improves vision and lowers the risk of macular degeneration, enhancing vision as we age. (I'm making this up—be sure to research whatever your backup statement is.)

Main Point: "Independent investing is crucial for comfort and security in retirement" (wealth). Share a prediction such as: there will be a Social Security shortfall beginning in 2037.

Main Point: "Listening is the most important element of conversation" (relationship). Offer a statistic about the percentage of teenagers who don't feel heard by their parents.

Main Point: "Understanding emotions leads to better sex" (sex). Quote an authority like LiveScience.com, which published an article stating that higher levels of self-esteem, autonomy, and empathy are associated with greater total sexual pleasure for women.

Main Point: "The jury's out on what makes a good parent" (identity). Offer testimonials of different parenting philosophies such as intuitive parenting, authoritative parenting, helicopter parenting, permissive parenting, instinctive parenting, empowerment parenting.

The *why* for my *main point* of this book is: When your *main point* is not clear, concise, and compelling, you lose your grip on the reader, he walks away, your message goes unheard, and you lose him as a prospect. If the reader doesn't know the importance of your *main point*, he won't be compelled to read on. If he stops reading, he will have nothing to remember you by. He'll have no reason to trust you. He won't follow your wisdom or use your product, and he will be doomed to his undesirable status quo.

When you lose your reader, you lose the opportunity to further engage, to close a sale, and to deliver value. If you don't deliver value, your business withers.

Knowing *why* gives us comfort. It validates our choices. It helps us proceed with confidence, security, and positive expectation. Not knowing *why* leaves us treading water without a compass and no shore in sight.

An engaging *why* drives your reader to drink in your wisdom, to benefit from your brilliance, and to engage your services. When he benefits from your service, he holds your reputation aloft by telling his friends, tweeting about it, and posting it on Facebook. Suddenly, doing business is easier and more profitable.

A Story of Knowing Why

My mother was Italian through and through, and my favorite meal as a kid was spaghetti with Mom's succulent, homemade Italian tomato sauce. She served the sauce and the macaroni from separate bowls, but prior to serving she always mixed a ladle full of sauce into the bowl of cooked pasta, turning the color of the noodles slightly orange instead of pasty white.

I didn't question it until I was served spaghetti at a friend's house. My friend's mom served the plain, white pasta on our plates, then topped it with a dollop of sauce without mixing the sauce into the noodles. I thought my friend's presentation was prettier. I liked the distinct contrast between the red sauce and the white pasta. I felt disappointment that my Mom—who hitherto in my eyes could do no wrong as an actual Italian person cooking Italian food— served it in a way that wasn't so pretty.

I asked Mom why she mixed in the sauce before serving. "It keeps the macaroni from getting gummy and sticking together," she said. Apparently, Mom preferred practical over pretty, and that redeemed her in my logic and in my heart. Knowing *why* gave me confidence to choose my own process (sauce in the noodles, please) when I was old enough to cook for myself.

WORK IT

Articulate *why*

Using your *main point* from the exercise in Chapter 1, construct your *why* by selecting (a) a Big 5 Concern to relate to your reader and (b) a presentation vehicle to support your premise.

YOUR MAIN POINT: _____

_____

Choose one of the Big 5 Concerns that will be affected if your reader ignores your Main Point.

THE BIG 5

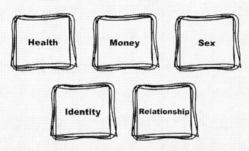

Health   Money   Sex

Identity   Relationship

Why is your *main point* crucial for your reader?

YOUR REASON WHY: _____

_____

Choose a vehicle to drive home your reason *why*.

        Quotation   Statistic

      Startling Fact   Prediction

          Comparison

Note the gist of your example here: _____

_____

_____

Humans are curious. We want to know why. If you have children, or if you've been around kids, or even if you remember being a kid, you've seen in action the natural tendency to ask why—and then why again, and why again. *How come? Why can't I? Why is it that color?* Knowing why is a desperate internal urge, and when it goes unmet we feel unsatisfied, frustrated, and insecure. *Why* gives us a platform. *Why* steadies us. *Why* motivates us to move forward and to grow. Give your reader the gift of *why*, and enjoy the ride to the next phase of relationship.

EASY STEP #3

Ramification
What's at Stake?

ram·i·fi·ca·tion, n.
3. ... outgrowth, consequence, complication
Webster's New Universal Unabridged Dictionary

What's the worst that could happen?

You've clearly conveyed your *main point.* You've stated a solid *why.* But even if the reader gets that it's important, she won't necessarily act on it. How many cases of "I've got to lose weight" have you seen go unaddressed until, alas, the doctor says lose weight or expect a massive coronary? People don't do something just because it's a good idea. It's not enough to point out their pain. You've got to make them *feel* it.

Remind your reader of the problem that drew her to you in the first place. Take her on a downward spiral, pointing out that ignoring the problem not only doesn't solve it, it makes it fester and get bigger. Show her how the unconscious habit of not addressing your *main point* holds her in a stagnant freeze-frame of (pick one: sloth, financial destitution, loneliness, frustration, anonymity, failure, unhappiness). Let her know her inaction renders her a powerless victim of circumstance.

Paint a bleak picture and associate it with one or more of the Big 5 Concerns identified in Easy Step #2. If she holds the status quo, what does she stand to lose? Will she lose sleep? Will she have a stroke? Will she lose her house? Will she go bankrupt? Will she be alone on Saturday night? Will her reputation be destroyed? Will she lose respect, confidence, her family?

Here's a sample using my *main point*, my reason *why*, and a projected scenario demonstrating the consequences of ignoring my sage advice:

> **Main Point**: Your *main point* must be clear, concise, and compelling.

> **Why**: When your *main point* is not clear, concise, and compelling, you lose your grip on the reader, she walks away, your message goes unheard, and you lose him as a prospect.

> **Ramification**: You lose a client, you lose a potential referral for future business, you put

your reputation at risk, and you add weight to the statistic about 8 out of 10 startups failing within 18 months.

Failure in business feels like failure as a person. *Why am I not good enough to succeed in business? Other people do it. What's the matter with me? Was I stupid even to try? What was I thinking?* This train of thought starts out small and builds in momentum until it's barreling headlong toward the precipice of no return.

Thoughts of insecurity, incapacity, self-belittlement, and inadequacy build as the tortuous tentacles of if-then devastation emerge. *If I'm bad at my business, then I must be a bad marketer, a bad money manager, a bad mother, a bad spouse, a bad person. No one wants me. I'm no good.*

In the downward spiral of negativity, physical symptoms appear: sour stomach, headache, tense muscles. Left unchecked as you dance on the edge of depression, minor ailments grow serious. Stomach pain becomes an ulcer, energy wanes, blood pressure goes askew. What started out as annoying soon becomes a legitimate physical threat, potentially manifesting as migraines, unhealthy weight, heart failure, or stroke.

In the skewed perspective that *I'm not worthy*, the very basic elements of life turn sour: health declines, finances dwindle, love life stagnates, friendships wane. When your *main point* is unclear and your reader doesn't see its importance, he stops paying attention. Your business withers and begins to dry up. You become physically lethargic, your thinking gets cloudy, your creativity is stunted, and you communicate ineffectively. Your beacon is dim, and new prospects no longer find you. Clients who were once faithful begin looking elsewhere. Your business fails.

You feel doomed to life on the streets!

OK, all that's a grave exaggeration, but you get the idea. Even better than painting an imaginary picture is to tell a true story that supports the consequences. Tell the story of someone who was offered your wisdom and the gloomy result because she chose not to act on it. Or tell your own story—what "disaster" befell you when you didn't follow your own advice?

Make the picture concrete. Show them how they keep getting the same results, caught in an unending loop like forgotten luggage on a conveyor belt. The scenery never changes but repeats itself to the point of predictable.

Please understand: as a life coach, my instinct is to stay upbeat, focus on the positive, and not dwell in the depths. This habit makes it challenging for me to take people down the negative pathway of doom, and I don't blame you if you don't want to go there either. But trust me, this process serves both you and your prospect very well. Just as you are her guide into the abyss, you will also be her guide to a brighter future.

Dr. Phil, in his book, *Life Strategies*, says, "If you're unwilling to acknowledge a thought, circumstance, problem, condition, behavior, or emotion—if you won't take ownership of your role in a situation—then you cannot and will not change it." Before you can guide them to the bright new beginning, they have to acknowledge the dissatisfaction of the status quo.

By emphasizing undesirable circumstances and the likelihood of future decline, you take the reader out of default mode, pique her awareness of what's missing, and spark the desire to do something to make life better. The realization that she can instigate change empowers her and inspires her to read on.

Here's my personal story of *ramification* using the *main point:* "Ask for the sale."

Ramification: Story of the Angel Client (Part I)

When I met with my first editing prospect (I call her my Angel Client, and you will soon see why), I offered her a three-page editing sample of my work and pointed out some of her table of contents listings that didn't align with her actual topic headings. I shortened some wordy parts and made her message more powerful. I complimented the strength and detail of her subject matter, and I pointed out that her personality did not show through. Her content read like a textbook, but as a reader I wanted to feel a personal connection. I wanted to feel like the author was talking *with* me rather than lecturing *at* me.

My Angel Client was thrilled with the changes and with my comments. I explained how I could do that for the whole manuscript and work with her to strengthen connection with the reader by bringing the voice of her heart into her words.[2]

And then I stopped. I waited silently for her to hire me.

---

[2] More on voice of the heart in Easy Step #5.

Going the extra mile, my Angel Client prodded me. "How much is your fee?" Flustered, I clumsily calculated out loud an hourly estimate based on out-of-thin-air word count, unsure how many decimal places my math might be off. I rounded the number one way or the other to name a flat fee for the project. She was on board.

But I didn't ask her for money.

You savvy business owners know that if you don't ask for money, you don't get money. But as someone who had spent most of my years as an employee, I didn't hold that concept front and center. Turns out if you don't ask for money, you lose the sale, and you lose respect. You breach trust. Your prospect walks away in confusion, taking with her your confidence and leaving you feeling inadequate. Not only do you lose this sale, you lose the possibility of future sales. You feel the agony of defeat. You spin your wheels trying to resurrect a career that's doomed for failure.

That's the *ramification* of not taking the step.

Stay tuned for the upbeat resolution to this story in Easy Step #4.

WORK IT

State the *ramifications*

Make a bullet list of potential consequences if the reader does not address your *main point*. List as many as you can: minor or major, physical or emotional, abstract or concrete, present or future. Paint the clear picture of how failure looks and feels.

This list of negative-feeling words, while not exhaustive, will get your juices flowing so that you can precisely convey the emotions your reader may experience if she does not follow your *main point* wisdom. The more specific you are in expressing your *ramifications*, the greater will be the impact on your reader.

Alone	Frustrated	Stagnant
Anxious	Guilty	Stressed
Ashamed	Hopeless	Trapped
Dependent	Inadequate	Unattractive
Depleted	Incompetent	Unclear
Devastated	Insecure	Underappreciated
Discouraged	Lethargic	Unhappy
Disrespected	Overwhelmed	Unqualified
Doubtful	Overworked	Unworthy
Embarrassed	Powerless	Weak
Fearful	Restricted	Worried
Fragmented	Scattered	Zapped

Congratulations! So far, you've articulated your *main point*, your *why*, and one or more *ramifications*. You've clarified for the reader where things have gone wrong until now, and you've painted the picture of what will happen if she preserves the status quo.

Philosophers report that history repeats itself—until someone breaks the cycle. Are you ready to offer the ray of hope that can break the cycle for your reader? Read on for the crucial next step.

EASY STEP #4

Vision
What's Possible?

Everything starts as somebody's daydream.
Larry Niven

Vision brings the future into now.

We want things because we think life will be better when we have them. It boils down to wanting to feel happier. *If I were just a little skinnier.... If I were a faster runner.... If I had more money.... If I were a better mom....*

The thing is, when we conjure the feeling of that outcome now, we energize ourselves to get the very thing we think we want. Help your reader shift his emotional set point from worry to enthusiasm, from doubt to positive expectation, from hard to easy by helping him visualize the dream as if it were already done. This ramps up his enthusiasm to take the next logical step toward his goal.

Imagination evokes feeling. Imagine your feet buried in warm sand and your body bathed in sunshine. Feel the warmth? Imagine you walk onto a stage, and before you even speak, the audience stands and applauds. Feel the validation, the satisfaction, the big wide smile? Imagine the delicious aroma of your favorite hot soup on a cold winter day. Feel the comfort, the security, the ease? Feels good, eh?

Now that you've brought your reader into the murky depths, your job is to pull him from the mire and plant him firmly in the fruitful garden of success. What will life be like after he implements his change? How will his life be different? What will your reader be, do, or have when he follows your lead, your program, and your wisdom?

This step is critical because we get what we think about. Picturing the problem already solved generates positive energy. It shifts the mindset from doubt to positive expectation and eager engagement. It creates momentum that generates the desired outcome. It gets you AND the client off the treadmill of same ol' same ol'.

Without this step, you both remain in limbo, swirling in a pool of confusion and uncertainty. Remember my Angel Client from Easy Step #3 who wanted to be published but had never been published before? She and her business were stuck in a holding pattern of low visibility. At that point in my editing career I had no client and had never had one. (Hey, we all have to start somewhere.) I was in a holding pattern of self-doubt, lack of confidence, and no income. My focus on my situation held me down. My Angel Client's focus on wanting to be published but not knowing how kept her frustrated and feeling incomplete.

Envisioning success propelled us both into action. We started small, first imagining how the book might impact her experience as a teacher and author. She anticipated a sense of completion, accomplishment, and legacy. Momentum grew more as we considered the outcome for her readers: feeling secure with a system that works; changing frustration to satisfaction; having more time, more energy, and more fun. And I envisioned the impact of her success on me: happy client, financial gain, established credibility, and satisfaction (both business and personal).

But we remained immobile because I didn't know how to ask for money and it scared me to death. She was ready to buy, but I was tongue-tied. I was afraid of rejection. Fortunately, my Angel Client's desire was strong.

Here's how the story resolved, complete with a bullet list offering a *vision* in relation to the story's *main point*.

Vision: Story of the Angel Client (Resolve)

My Angel Client (bless her heart!) pleaded with me to guide her. "Tell me what to do! Do you want a deposit? Do I pay in full? How do we seal this deal?" I was so naïve that I hadn't thought it through. I had in mind that I would send her an invoice after our conversation, but she wanted to seal the deal then and there.

I once heard a creative gentleman describe five-year-olds playing soccer and doing what he called the "doughnut dance." The little players run like crazy toward the ball, but when they get there, they are afraid to kick it, so they dance around it, never actually touching the ball. My Angel Client was ready to give me money if only I would ask. I was doing the doughnut dance. I couldn't bring myself to kick that ball. She was frustrated, and so was I.

Noting my incapacity to speak, my Angel Client asked, "How much do you want? A hundred dollars? Fifty percent?" I felt a surge of relief. It was like being on stage, forgetting my lines, and being saved by a cue card. It was all I could do not to assault her with a bear hug of gratitude. In humble

appreciation for this angel who walked
me through my first selling experience,
I stepped up to the plate and asked for a
hundred dollars. She wrote me a check.

We both felt relief at this resolution. We
got unstuck. We no longer floundered in
an eddy of uncertainty. We felt confident,
secure, in sync, with positive expectation
that good things were ahead. We were both
empowered and ready to take action. My
client (no longer a prospect!) helped me ditch
the doughnut dance and put the ball into
play. I took ownership of my capacity as a
professional editor, ready to do what I love
most: play with words. It was a win-win.

After my Angel Client suggested I request a deposit,
the atmosphere changed:

- She handed me money.
- She felt relief, knowing she had commandeered the
  desired service.
- I felt relief, knowing I had a client.
- She was eager to begin her rewrites and get them
  to me for final edit.
- I was eager to do what I love: take good content
  and make it clear, concise, and compelling.
- She felt energized.
- I felt energized.

- I felt legitimate.
- We forged a bond, personal and professional, that enriched each of us.
- My freelance editing career was off and running.
- She felt productively engaged.
- I felt successful.

How do you paint a picture of success?

Henry DeVries of Indie Books International (http://indiebooksintl.com/) says to tell a hero/villain/mentor story. Begin the story showing the reader as the hero. The hero has a problem—the villain—that holds him back. Your *ramification* demonstrates the problem in great detail. This begs for intervention and rescue. Enter the mentor (i.e., you), who guides the hero to the land of happily ever after.

Science fiction writer Larry Niven said, "Everything starts as somebody's daydream." I say there are two kinds of dreamers. One focuses on how hard things are to accomplish, and one imagines how life will be when it's already done. Both kinds of dreamers can get the job done, it's just that one way feels icky and one feels fun. My own tale of writing and publishing two different books demonstrates the power of focus.

A Tale of Two Publishings

Early in my career as a life coach, I perceived that I had no credibility. I had earned the Certified Professional

Coach certificate from the Academy for Coach Training, fulfilling the certification requirements of the International Coach Federation. But my post-high school education consisted of a one-year legal secretarial course. I didn't feel worthy to coach people who had college degrees. How could they possibly see me as an expert? It was my dream to write a book so that people would take me seriously. Without a book, I felt doomed to fail.

Using Henry DeVries's formula, in this story I am the heroine (aka dreamer); the villain is my thought pattern, my doubts and anxieties about the monumental task of becoming a published author; and I relied on myself as mentor. (Spoiler alert—this doesn't play out well for me.)

As Tale of Publishing #1 opens, the dreamer (me) faces the villain of her own negative thinking: "It's too hard!" She wallows in:

- This is complicated!
- I don't know where to start.
- What are the rules?
- Who will design it?
- What about the cover?
- How does it get printed?
- Do I need an editor?
- Should I self-publish?
- What if it doesn't work?
- I'm pressured by deadlines (self-imposed, mind you).

- What if I can't?
- So many details—no time to write!
- What if nobody likes it?
- What if I fail?

Linger for a minute on these negative thoughts. How do they make you feel? For me, it stripped any shred of glamour from the journey from writer to published author. These thoughts were heavy baggage that weighed me down. I felt worried, overwhelmed, and inadequate. On an emotional scale of 1 to 10, where 1 is despair and 10 is exhilaration and passion, these thoughts felt no better than 3 or 4. From this emotional state the steps were burdensome and difficult. Eeeewww.

EMOTIONAL SCALE

10	Passion/Exhilaration/Freedom
9	Enthusiasm
8	Positive Expectation
7	Optimism
6	Contentment
5	Frustration
4	Overwhelm
3	Doubt/Worry
2	Anger/Blame
1	Fear/Despair

This emotional setting of 3 or 4 is typical for the problem-focused dreamer. The load feels heavy and out of balance. It fed my doubts and called my capability into question.

Author Matt Sumell describes his experience of writing *Making Nice*: "I can't and won't deny that parts of it are deeply personal, that it was emotionally expensive for me to write." I, too, felt that emotional expense in my writing and publishing. I needed a way to change *expensive* to *expansive*.

I did finally publish the book, *Full Bloom: 7 Practical Steps to Get What You Want +1 to Grow On*. There! Spent, exhausted, and still feeling it wasn't good enough, I didn't bother with a celebratory launch. I did nothing to actively market it or promote it. I spoke quietly of it and hoped it would magically draw clients to me all by itself.

The missing piece for me was the mentor. (Remember, you are the mentor for your reader.) This demonstrates Easy Step #3, *ramification*. My process actually kept me mired in negativity, at a 3 to 4 on the Emotional Scale. I admit to an emotional spike when I held that first book in my hand; but the next question was *now what?* and I had no clue how to answer it. The feeling of success quickly waned because the whole process was fueled with worry and doubt.

Enter Anna Goldsworthy, my business buddy and cofounder of Wisdom Well Retreats. In partnership we offered self-discovery retreats for women based on powerful, thought-provoking questions to spark self-awareness. We faithfully posted a new Question of the Week on our website, and after a few months Anna suggested we could compile the questions into a book. "Wouldn't that be fun!" she said.

Fun? Did she say *fun?* I still felt raw from the grueling, painful process of writing and publishing the first book. I was reluctant (at best) to embark on that journey again.

Anna pointed out that we already had the material. All we had to do was compile our weekly questions, plump it up with a little quip for each, and add some simple, practical tools. It could be a course manual for our retreats. Our premise was that women could feel good no matter what, so why not apply that feel-good principle to the book-writing process?

Thank you, Anna, my mentor! Already I felt relief— no pressure, no hurry; just have fun.

I embarked on Tale of Publishing #2 by closing my eyes. Instead of dwelling on the fear-based thoughts from my first experience, I deliberately imagined that the process was already done and that I had lots to celebrate:

- The book feels so good in my hands!
- I love seeing my name on the cover!
- People respect me!
- People recognize my name!
- I get paid handsomely to speak!
- Experts in my field use my book in their practice.
- Publishing houses have bidding wars for my work.

- I get a six-figure advance for the sequel!
- I quit my day job.
- My kids FINALLY take me seriously!
- I feel confident.
- I feel energized, worthy, credible.
- I feel validated, productive, satisfied.
- People thank me for inspiring them.
- I'm leaving a valuable legacy!

Linger for a leisurely moment on each of these positive thoughts. Do you feel lighter and freer? Are you dancing your way up the Emotional Scale from 3 or 4 (worry and doubt) to 8 or 9 (positive expectation and eager engagement)? I felt like I'd left my baggage behind and sprouted wings. From this emotional state my actions were backed with clarity, energy, and forward momentum. I'd shifted from *have to* to *want to*, which made each successive step more efficient, productive, and fun!

Worrier or Dreamer?

IT'S TOO HARD!

I don't know how.

It costs too much.

What if it doesn't work?

I don't have enough time!

What if nobody likes it?

What if I fail?

IT'S ALREADY DONE!

It feels GOOD to be DONE!

People respect me!

Clients are lined up at my door!

Experts call me an authority!

Even my KIDS respect me!

This is easy!

WORK IT

Ditch the baggage and don your wings

If you took time to linger on the negative phrases, I'm betting you spiraled down into "why bother?" Draw a rectangle around the list of negative thoughts in the previous illustration. Now draw a handle at the top of the rectangle. This is your baggage.

If you took time to linger on the positive phrases, you probably felt the upward spiral into lightness, freedom and ease. Draw an oval around the list of positive thoughts in the illustration above. Now attach wings to the oval. These wings are your ticket to success.

Leave your baggage at the gate and let your dreams take flight!

The beauty of this process is that it can be applied to any endeavor, not just to writing a book. In fact, the book we birthed using this process, *Feel Good No Matter What,* is filled with thought-provoking prompts and tools to help you shift from baggage to wings on 52 different topics.

The *vision* of possibility sparks action for positive change. Portray your reader as the hero of his story, seeking relief from the pain that keeps him stuck. Be the mentor who offers a clear, positive *vision* and whisks him away to the healing elixir—your unique solution.

Help your reader leave his baggage at the gate and let his dreams take flight. He will be compelled to read on to discover the priceless value you have to offer.

A vision for you

Imagine that your *main point* is so clear that it almost runs as a mantra in your mind. It is so concise that your reader has no chance to get bored, and it is so profound that it inspires him to read on. With your clarity you have made him feel secure in your wisdom and expertise. He wants to drink more of your magic potion, and when he does, he is certain he has found the elixir to cure his ails. He engages with you for mutual fun and profit. His problem is solved, his life vastly improves, his attitude shifts upward on the Emotional Scale, he finds the love of his dreams. He soars on a cloud of success held aloft by your wisdom. He spreads the word, plastering praise for you on all the social media sites, and soon you're keeping a waiting list of enthusiastic prospects. You have found the key to passive income. Your business nearly runs itself, and you spend more time on warm, sunny beaches with the people you love the most. Life is good!

Read on for Easy Step #5 and learn how to solidify your relationship with your readers and your clients.

EASY STEP #5

Vulnerability
Speak with the Voice of Your Heart

What we know matters, but who we are matters more.
Brené Brown

I've come to what I know through a good deal of research and self-education. But my greatest insights and true knowledge have come from the mundane and profound elements of day-to-day living. On exposure to each circumstance, viewpoint, person, or element, who I am has shifted.

I've spent angst-ridden years in the teeth-gritting need to be right. I've strived to meet Dad's expectations of perfection. I've judged and questioned myself, my work product, and my own worthiness. I've read all the self-help books and done all the exercises, endeavoring to let go of attachment, self-judgment, and the thought that I'm not good enough. As I related in the Easy Step #4 story about baggage and wings, I've learned that holding on to tension, angst, and worry restricts me, restricts my story, restricts my process, and restricts my outcome (not to mention my income!). And the devastating *ramification* is that it restricts my happiness.

I am also blessed to have glimpsed success in letting go, shifting viewpoint, and having a better, happier journey the second time around. I am hopeful that my story can help you find your way from stress to success, from worry to woohoo, from bondage to freedom. But I don't pretend it's easy, and I make no guarantees.

Voice of the heart

We all have a soft, fragile underbelly. Life is risky, and we are vulnerable. It's easy to believe that if we keep our flaws hidden, people will love us more. But concealment increases pressure, builds intensity, and dims the light of who we really are.

I encourage you to speak with the voice of your heart, share your vulnerable truth, and connect with the hearts of your readers.

What exactly is *vulnerability* and how do we express it? *Vulnerability* is susceptibility to physical or emotional attack. How can being vulnerable possibly work to your advantage, especially as you speak to perfect strangers in writing with an aim to appear as an expert? *Vulnerability,* my friend, opens the door to trust.

I've learned that people will forget what you said,
people will forget what you did, but people will
never forget how you made them feel.

Maya Angelou

People remember how you make them feel. *Vulnerability* is the language of the heart. When you speak your truth from your heart, others see you in relation to themselves. You forge a commonality. Whether the commonality is negative (pain, frustration, embarrassment) or positive (humor, enthusiasm, joy), commonality feels comfortable. The reader sees you as a kindred spirit, someone who gets her. She belongs to your club. She hears you speaking *to her* as if you are face to face over coffee, not *at her* as if you are behind a podium. *Vulnerability* is wearing your heart on your sleeve. As Brené Brown says, "Imperfections are not inadequacies; they are reminders that we're all in this together."

When I try to convince you of the rightness of my opinion, I erect a separation barrier. The unspoken subtext is *you are wrong and I am right.* But when I show you I share and understand your humor or your pain, the barrier dissolves. Now you are ready to hear me.

Say I'm writing an article promoting the concept of tough love. I can cite statistics and facts that show it's effective. I can quote experts. And I can be adamant in the expression of my opinion. But numbers and quotes and scientific references don't touch the emotions. They serve a purpose, but without the emotional component, they leave my reader cold and separate.

What if, instead, I tell you that the hardest thing I ever did was take the keys from my 18-year-old son and tell him he couldn't live with us anymore because it only enabled his drug habit? This is a critical, highly emotional, personal story for me. It's my truth, and I'm trusting you with it. That evokes empathy. We all have stories, and they all have different details, but the fact that I share mine allows you to take me seriously, to trust me, to believe me, to empathize with me. It makes me real.

Two layers of vulnerability

Using the voice of the heart to expose my fragile underbelly has a surface value and a deeper value. Surface: the story that I tell puts my flaws and failures and weaknesses on the table for all to see. In this view (on the table in front of us) the flaws and weaknesses are separate from me. Deeper: that I even tell the story puts *me* on the table, at the mercy of the reader to accept not just my flaws, but also the core of who I really am.

Foster trust and connection

Vulnerability conveys trust and fosters connection. Nothing makes someone trust you more than your own trust in them. Tell your truth. Your readers will see you as sensitive and fallible, and they will trust you to honor equally their sensitivities and fallibilities.

> *I define connection as the energy that exists between people when they feel seen, heard, and valued; when they can give and receive without judgment; and when they derive sustenance and strength from the relationship.*
>
> Brené Brown

Without trust, your reader has no reason to move forward with you. By not engendering trust, you tip the scale for mistrust, which is a surefire impetus for your reader to turn tail and run.

A Story of Vulnerability

As I moved from my Angel Client to deeper waters, I was introduced to a publisher who farms out the editing portion of her projects. This opened for me a potentially greater pool of editing work than seeking out authors one at a time. The only thing I had going for me was an introduction from someone I'd met casually two or three times at networking events, so she didn't have first-hand experience of my work.

In my deep past I would have agonized over how I could present myself to this publisher. I would have tried to gloss over the fact that I was brand new to the game as a professional, and I may have tried to cobble an old, irrelevant testimonial into something that sounded snazzy and important. I would have looked for ways to bling up my resumé to look like I had a great backlog of experience. In reality, my practical experience was subtle, almost secondary to my primary skill as a legal word processor.

Instead, I went with *Vulnerability*. I told the publisher my truth: that I had only recently decided to freelance. I told her my guiding principle (keep it simple), my core value (crystal clear communication), and my passion (playing with words to change ho-hum to zowie).

I love to edit—I do it almost compulsively. I love communication that is clear, concise, and compelling. In fourth grade I knew instinctively how to diagram sentences, and I saw almost no value in that because I found it so easy. The knowledge felt incidental, as if it were a given. I knew how sentences worked in the same way I knew that walking was more expedient than crawling. I found it inconceivable that everyone didn't get it. As a consequence, it never occurred to me until much later in life that I could make a career out of editing sentences for others.

After some life experience, I know the value of nurturing what comes with ease and feels good. I am in my element when I'm editing. I often say, "I write gooder than I talk," because speaking with clarity the first time out is a challenge for me. Truth be told, my writing is equally as clumsy as my speech, but editing gives me a do-over. I take great satisfaction in condensing a bulky 20-word sentence into eight words that foster clarity, enhance impact, and ease reader fatigue.

The publisher offered me a manuscript on the spot in a genre I love the most, fully trusting me. She even helped me with what to charge in a way that is simple, lucrative, and within industry standards. I loved the project, I gave it my all, and I reduced 67,000 loosely combined words to 55,000 solid-fit words that packed a powerful punch. All parties were satisfied, and I now have a trusted resource for editing referrals.

Find your stories

How do you find the stories to demonstrate your *vulnerability?*

When I tried to come up with powerful stories, my life felt normal and uneventful. I had lived a boring existence, accustomed to my day-to-day experience, and I could see nothing extraordinary or special worth telling. I'd suffered no catastrophes worthy of gaining empathy. I hadn't been run over by a truck. I wasn't born with a disability. I hadn't had a near-death experience. I wasn't physically abused or poverty stricken.

To find my stories (turns out there were multiple—who knew?) I journaled. By *journal* I mean the physical act of writing with pen and paper, not using a keyboard or electronics.

In her book *The Artist's Way—A Spiritual Guide to Higher Creativity*, Julia Cameron recommends what she calls "morning pages", amounting to three pages of longhand stream-of-consciousness writing to facilitate "brain drain". The function of brain drain is to sweep away the mental clutter that prohibits the free flow of creativity. I've personally indulged in her practice and find something magical in the three-page requirement. At first, it's hard to even come up with something to say. Then the rambling begins, and by the time the third page comes around, words and ideas are flowing with more clarity, meaning, and purpose.

Two common myths about journaling—debunked

Before you shake your head in resistance, let me shoot down some common lame excuses not to journal.

I don't have time. I have a book to write. Your desire to write the book is the very reason not to skip this process. You wouldn't run a marathon without training first. Pen-and-paper journaling trains you to write and to speak your truth. It exercises your communication muscles and taps into your genius. Buried beneath the cloudy clutter of mental drivel are the gems of wisdom that will serve you and your readers. Give it a try. You already don't have the book published. What have you got to lose?

Longhand is labor intensive and time consuming. I'll use the keyboard—it's faster. Here's the thing about that. Using a keyboard engages the logical, analytical, objective, data-driven left brain. This is useful when you want to capture details and determine logistics and keep score. On the other hand, the physical action of using pen and paper engages the intuitive, holistic, subjective, creative right brain and taps the well of ideas, concepts, and connections that evoke personal "aha" moments and wow your reader. Use the keyboard for data and details and to transcribe what you've written in longhand. Use pen and paper to clear mental and emotional clutter and tap into creativity.

In my own journaling, seven stories emerged to illustrate some of my challenges and what I learned or became because of them:

1. I grew up as an Air Force brat, moving every two to four years in my K-to-12 years. I experienced the heartbreak of losing touch with close friends, and I was challenged to make new friends and to adapt to a variety of cultural and geographic changes. Result: **I am flexible and adaptable.**

2. As an only child, I spent much of my formative years with adults. I received high praise for following direction, being quiet, not being "obnoxious," and not embarrassing myself or my family. This resulted in a deep-rooted fear of speaking, singing, dancing, or having an opinion that conflicted with another. My resulting belief that held me back: **I'm not good enough.**

3. My adult experience includes juggling and prioritizing multiple phone lines, multiple schedules, and document production for multiple attorneys to meet multiple deadlines. Concurrently with that I maintained the household for my husband and our three boisterous boys, each with unique talents, challenges, and idiosyncrasies. Consequence: **I'm a good manager and multitasker.**

4. At the age of sixteen I soloed an airplane (my first solo flight) in a 35-mph crosswind. This speaks to my **willingness to take risks and my strong ability to focus.**

5. In five minutes I coached a speaker to transform from noncontender to winner-take-all in a high-stakes speaking contest. She walked away with $13,000. **I'm good in the clutch.**

6. Not so long ago my father took his life by gunshot to the head. (Stay tuned—I'm sure there's a whole separate book around that.) The jolt triggered a shift of awareness for me, suddenly revealing that everything I had considered to be his faults were,

in reality, his strengths. **Now I know how to step back from the detail and see the big picture.**

7. In my position as receptionist and office manager I kept track of comings and goings of attorneys. One particular lawyer would come out of his office to my desk (me being the only one he could justify interrupting). His untiring opening line was, "You know what I hate?" He would proceed to rant about some perceived political or personal injustice, and it made me tired. One day when he came out of his office, I beat him to the opener and asked, "What do you love today?" It changed his focus, disposition, and energy, and I was delighted to listen to him. **This reveals my gift for guiding conversation to shift energy from negative to positive.**

I share all of this for the sake of example. As you journal and unveil the stories that make you tick, put them somewhere handy so you can pull them out in perfect timing. Depending on the nature of your audience and topic, you will choose one or two specific vignettes that are relevant for your reader.

Each of these stories speaks to my style, my personality, my values system, and my guiding principles. This helps my reader know me, relate to me, and easily decide whether to engage with me.

When I tell my Tale of Two Publishings, it supports my self-proclamation:

You know how independent business owners struggle to stand out in a crowd? From my experience of writing and publishing books from two completely different perspectives, and from my personal experience of abandoning my heavy baggage to sprout wings of freedom, I can show the audience how to let go of what doesn't serve them—in their process and on the page—so they can get published and be noticed with ease!

What is your self-proclamation?

WORK IT

Speak with the voice of your heart

Use the timeline below to mark key times/events in your life that have affected your actions and your decisions or that have evoked your passions or your fears.

Key things may be words someone said, a circumstance, a traumatic event, a moment of "aha" or discovery, an experience, an accomplishment, a "failure," an influential book, or a chance encounter.

Give particular thought to how each key element triggered an internal shift for you by changing your perspective, calling on your strength, confirming your passion, or revealing your fear.

Birth‹-----|-----|-----|-----|-----|-----|-----|-----|-----›

For each incident on your timeline, tell your story. You can use this simple formula if you like:

Once upon a time …. (begin with you in your ordinary world)

Every day …. (describe the same old problem you faced)

Then one day …. (tell of the key circumstance/person/event)

Suddenly …. (describe your shift of perspective/new wisdom/etc.)

Ever since then …. (reveal the new you/why you now do what you do)

Opening your heart to the reader opens the reader's heart to receive your grace and your wisdom. It primes him to trust you, to befriend you, to relate to you, to appreciate you, to release fear of you. It gives him hope that he, too, can overcome and work through his challenges. It makes it easy for him to do business with you.

Find the voice of your heart. Know it, hear it, acknowledge it. Connect it with the value and strengths it represents for you. Let down your barrier, and share it with your reader.

The fruit of heart-to-heart connection ripens your reader to receive the *value* you are about to offer in Easy Step #6.

EASY STEP #6

Value
Give a Gift

It is the service we are not obliged to give that people value most.
James Cash Penney

With Easy Steps #1 through #5 you've laid the groundwork for your reader. You've told her *what,* you've told her *why* it's important, you've explained the *ramification* if things remain status quo, and you've painted a rosy *vision* of how life will be once she makes your recommended change. You've taken her from bleak to blissful, and you've bared your fragile underbelly by speaking with the voice of your heart.

But so far all of that is intangible. Sure, she's feeling euphoric, and that's priceless. She was looking to feel good, and you delivered the feeling.

Now deliver *value* she can hold in her hand.

According to *Webster's New Universal Unabridged Dictionary*, *value* means "impact of meaning; force; significance; a quality that renders something desirable or useful; intrinsic excellence and desirability."

The first five Easy Steps have captured your reader's attention, and she is champing at the bit to receive something juicy. Give it to her!

You've held the reins and led her down the path. If you don't deliver something of value, you risk breaching her trust. When you offer her something useful, she feels good (remember, that's ultimately what she wants), her faith in you is supported, and she's willing to travel further down the road with you. This bears repeating with emphasis: *She's willing to travel further down the road WITH YOU.*

Surely, she loved holding the *vision* you painted for her in Easy Step #4, but all the daydreaming in the world won't move her into action. If you leave her in daydream mode, she may lounge there indefinitely, never moving forward. If that happens, her dream fizzles, and she slips quickly, if quietly, back to the very rut she seeks to escape. She tosses your book on a pile of others that she perceived would answer her prayer, leaving a sour taste in her mouth. She sloughs back into immobility, which she interprets as failure, and she blames you for deserting her.

DO NOT LET THIS HAPPEN!

Put her into action. Action lubricates stuck gears so the engine of creativity can purr happily along.

A journey of a thousand miles begins with a single step.
Lao Tzu

Without action, self-help becomes shelf-help. Inspire success by suggesting action. If you offer a tip, a process, or an exercise and your reader tries it, even if he fails, his active engagement starts a momentum that leads to more ideas and action. Even if he abandons your specific action for one of his own, your work is successful because you have sparked his unique style, and he is bound to find success. Your gift not only makes him feel good (bonus for him), it also generates his creative energy. His action sparks his creativity and taps into his genius. This makes him feel successful, and because of your valuable tip, he will associate you with his success.

Offering *value* tells your reader not only that you are in the trench with him, but also that you trust him to put that value to his own best use. It's like walking the child to kindergarten on the first day, assuring him you know where he's headed, leading him to the door, introducing him to the teacher, and then letting go of his hand so he can explore the new world in his own way.

Make your gift a simple action step that is relevant and doable.

The easier it is, the more successful your reader will feel.

Here are some easy ways to deliver *value*:

- Give step-by-step how-to instructions.
- Offer a top-10 list.
- Outline a procedure.
- Provide a checklist.
- Deliver an informative report.
- Give a tip or tool to simplify a process.
- Display a chart or image to clarify understanding.
- Offer a cutout of pocket tips to be carried in a wallet or used as a bookmark.

You may be thinking it feels risky to release trade secrets when the reader hasn't even hired you yet. Not to worry. Giving a useful tool doesn't require you to give away the farm. But offer *value* substantial enough to make her feel well armed to fight her battle. It reveals your wisdom and expertise about the farm and lets the reader see you as a valuable resource with a lush crop of more stuff she wants. That puts you in a place of fond affection and respect, and it secures your status as an expert.

When you give *value* that is relevant to her desired outcome, she sees you as the source and knows where to come for more.

WORK IT

Wrap up your gift

Make a list of critical elements for your clients' success. For each element, write a one-line tip or devise a simple exercise that will help anchor that element and spur them into action.

Don't feel compelled to offer everything on your list. Select something that is relevant in the context of your chapter or book.

Print up each of the other gifts on separate index cards or business cards and pass them out in face-to-face meetings. Our book, *Feel Good No Matter What,* carries the thread of ten simple tips to release resistance and feel good. We created a bookmark that promotes the book on one side and lists tips to feel good on the other. It's an offering of *value* and a step above a business card in so many ways!

Read on for Easy Step #6, solidifying your relationship with your readers and your clients.

EASY STEP #7

Invitation
Offer a Simple Call to Action

The great aim of education is not knowledge but action.
Herbert Spencer

You've stated your case for the reader. You've drawn a distinction between sticking with the status quo and living the dream. You've given valuable ideas and resources and processes. You've spoken from your heart to expose the tender underbelly of your own challenges or shortcomings. You've forged a relationship with your reader, and it's time to make a play date.

Your book or written material should not only offer value to the reader, it should also offer value for you in the form of lead generation and business income. Your book gives you visibility and credibility. It's your ticket to land speaking gigs and get in front of people who want what you dish up. Remember the story from Easy Steps #3 and #4: *Ask for the sale.* Invite your reader to move forward in a way that will benefit you both.

An *invitation* is a call to action. Without a call to action, your relationship with the reader ends when she closes the book. If this happens, you're back to scrounging for clients. Offer a strong call to action and boost your business.

Your written message holds an inherent promise: that the reader's life or experience will be enhanced by the new wisdom or product that you promote. But the power of the new element is lost if not put to use. A call to action says *come play with me so I can help you succeed.* The reader's success contributes to your success.

Empower the reader to change her experience, and you elevate her self-esteem, confidence, and success. Knowing the effect of diet and exercise on physical well-being is useless if it is not put into action. The reader reads your material in hopes of improving her health, advancing her career, finding financial comfort, or living a happier lifestyle. An action step puts her on the path of success.

No matter what you're writing—a book, a report, a flier, a letter, a blog—make your *invitation* clear, concise, compelling, and simple. *Simple* means: offer a single step that is easy to take.

Sample *invitations* for a marketing piece:

- Call this number for more information.
- E-mail to schedule an appointment.
- Click to enroll.
- Click to receive a free gift (make it valuable!).
- Order now.
- Join a webinar.
- Subscribe to your newsletter.
- Attend an event.

Sample *invitations* for a chapter end:

- Do this exercise to practice the principles of this chapter.
- Take this quiz to anchor the learning.
- Take this action to prepare for the coming chapter.

Be sure your end-of-chapter *invitation* stands a good chance of success for the reader so that it fuels the desire to read the next chapter.

> **Sample *invitations* for the end of a book, a report, or a speech:**
>
> - Register for a class.
> - Make an appointment.
> - Buy a product.
> - Order the next book.
> - Purchase a ticket.

Begin with the end in mind.

Stephen R. Covey

Know before you go! In *The 7 Habits of Highly Effective People*, Stephen Covey talks about the principle that all things are created twice. First we think and design, and then we put hands on to build. Know your call to action before you write your chapter, report, book, or article. Knowing what your *invitation* will be is like having a blueprint to keep your content focused, on task, and relevant.

WORK IT

List 10 possible calls to action that might move your reader to connect with you.

_____

_____

_____

_____

_____

_____

_____

_____

_____

_____

Put a checkmark by your top three favorites.

Choose **ONLY one** to offer for a specific book, article, or marketing piece.

"But I have so many options—how do I choose?"

I get that it's tempting to offer more than one opportunity to connect. It seems like having more choices is better. Not so. Too many choices can paralyze your prospect, which leads to procrastination, which leads, ultimately, to no decision. Resist the urge! Make it easy.

 TIP Use two criteria to choose the right *invitation* for the job:
1. Your intention.
2. Your feeling.

Intention. Is your intention to build your list? To add to your revenue stream? To get a referral? To expand your visibility? To make a personal connection?

Feeling. When you imagine your reader taking this step, do you have mixed emotions: *Oh boy, she said yes! Oh no, now I have to work hard to follow through!* Or do you feel solid enthusiasm: *Oh boy, she said yes, and now we get to play!*

Choose what feels best in support of your intention.

My intention for this book is to increase my stream of editing clientele. I could invite my readers to

- Send me a 3-page writing sample
- Join my mailing list
- Hire me to speak to your group

- Buy my books
- Attend my workshop
- Schedule a strategy session

I thrive on personal connection, so my favorite offer is to schedule a strategy session to see if we are a fit.

You can request a strategy session right now by going to <u>www.ninadurfee.com</u>

To help you decide whether you want to risk that step with me, read on for Easy Step #8.

EASY STEP #8

Investment

**Fan the Ember of Promise
into the Blaze of Success**

Because I'm worth it.
L'Oréal

You know what it means to invest. You've invested time and money to build your business. You've honed your skills, you've researched your competition, and you've devised the processes that work for you. You've spent countless hours building a website, designing marketing materials, printing business cards, and attending networking groups and industry conventions and seminars. You've invested good money for your education, office equipment and supplies, physical space to conduct business, and wear and tear on your car. Maybe you've hired employees and accountants and lawyers. You have invested time and hard work and money for business success. You are committed!

Has it been a walk in the park? Was the seed money dropped in your lap? Did it all happen as easily as you'd hoped? Have you ever lost sleep worrying where the next client will come from? Are you satisfied with the status quo, or would you like a higher rate of return?

What if you could boost your business without boosting your sweat and effort?

The effect of all the time and money you spend on your business fizzles if your message doesn't engage your prospect. The previous 7 Easy Steps go a long way to magnetizing your message. Easy Step # 8—*investment*—is the anchor that perfects your message. But you've already invested so much time and effort and money. What else can you invest in that doesn't zap you mentally, physically, and emotionally and still offers a great return on your investment?

Professional editing

With respect to a manuscript (or any written material, for that matter), editing is the act of revising or correcting. Most writers do a good deal of editing even as they write, deleting or rearranging text, correcting misspellings or typos, rephrasing for clarity. If you've done that already, why bother to hire a professional?

The myth

If you think that because you have a degree in English or creative writing you don't need an editor, think again. No matter how good the writer, a professional editor will improve the product, and here's why: Writers are too close to their work.

I've seen this topic addressed over and over in a multitude of writers' forums. We are so intent on our message that the mechanics of language slip by unnoticed. As we edit our own work, we are biased by knowing what we mean to say. In their book *Made to Stick: Why Some Ideas Survive and Others Die*, Chip and Dan Heath talk about the "curse of knowledge". The idea is that the more you know, the worse you become at communicating your knowledge. They're talking about conveying concepts and ideas (say, from an expert to a lay person), but the concept also applies to an editor reading her own work.

Nothing drove this point home more clearly for me than when I launched the ninadurfee.com website to promote my editing services. I agonized over the content for each page, the layout, the color scheme, the logo, the links. Eager to get on with my business, I skipped the step of hiring an editor, and I published the site. The first person who looked at it told me I had misspelled *author* on the home page. Sheesh! I knew so well what I intended to say that I assumed I'd said it. Even though my eyes passed over that word hundreds of times, I was blinded, duped by an optical illusion of my own devise.

The opposite end of that stick is the tendency to overexplain. In an effort to be sure the reader understands fully, writers often repeat themselves, expressing their point in so many different ways that the reader tires, loses interest, and shouts, "I get it, already!" Give your reader the respect she deserves. Credit her with common sense, literacy, and the capacity to interpret clearly expressed content. And remember, people have short attention spans. They don't want to waste time in a repetitive loop.

So the writer who breeds more words than he needs,
is making a chore for the reader who reads.

Dr. Seuss

A good editor offers the benefit of a fresh set of eyes and a different baseline of understanding. What you assume to be true about your craft or product may not be obvious to your prospect, and a good editor will flesh out places where you haven't been specific enough, as well as places you can pare down to make your ideas fully digestible.

Good editing gets rid of the fluff and showcases your genius in the best light possible. Professional editing makes your creativity and wisdom palatable for the reader.

Consider clothing. The fact that I work at home in my yoga pants, tank top, and flip-flops doesn't affect my talent, wisdom, or expertise. But if I want a group of executives to take me seriously, I'm better off to show up in traditional business garb. Think of good editing as the proper attire for your message. It doesn't make you any smarter, but it definitely makes you more credible, and it makes your wisdom more palatable.

Clear expression and quality editing ensure an enjoyable experience for the reader and eliminate reader fatigue. The reader understands your message when it is written well and edited for consistency, clarity, and correctness. If either your message or the way you express it is murky, your reader will scratch his head in confusion. If he can't make sense of your ideas, he won't relate to you as an expert. If he has to struggle to understand you, he won't benefit from your expertise, and he won't pursue your product or service.

What, exactly, does editing consist of? In the satirical words of Mark Twain, "Writing is easy. All you have to do is cross out the wrong words." Were it only that simple....

Here are four ways an editor can help:

Copyediting: Focuses on mechanical issues at the sentence and paragraph level, including:

- Grammar
- Punctuation
- Spelling
- Style
- Sentence and paragraph structure
- Vocabulary usage
- Consistency in capitalization, punctuation, numbers, hyphenation, abbreviation, etc.

Structural or technical editing: Focuses on language issues and organization of existing content, including:

- Smoothing transitions
- Reorganizing content, tightening and rephrasing, trimming unnecessary fat
- Suggesting rewrites for clarity, readability, and flow
- Tuning to your voice and how your reader will connect with you
- Noting repetition of overused words
- Flagging names, dates, sources, etc., for fact-checking by the author
- Confirming that your book's overarching principle is met with the content of every chapter or segment

Developmental editing: Developmental editing runs deeper than structural or technical editing. For nonfiction it often occurs early in the process and may include refining an outline and checking for strategic order of presentation. Developmental editing for fiction pays attention to characterization, plotting and pacing, organization and structure, voice and tone, literary devices, and stylistic elements.

Proofreading: Proofreading happens after completion of developmental editing, structural editing, and copyediting. Proofreading is typically performed on an actual printed proof of the book (not your electronic or typed manuscript). It's good to have more than one round of proofreading: order a book, proofread, make corrections; order another book, proofread, make corrections, until you are satisfied.

Good editing renovates shoddy sentence structure, separates and eliminates the chaff, amplifies your voice, changes ordinary to compelling. Good editing helps you speak less and say more with clarity, concreteness, and connectivity.

A good editor will save you the embarrassment and complication of aftermath retractions and apologies. A good editor will help elevate your credibility, your reputation, and your business. Interview editors until you find one you connect with, someone who enjoys reading the genre you write and who will perform the services you want.

Invest in a good editor to dress your message for success. You're worth it!

8 Critical Questions to Answer
before You Hire an Editor

1. **Whom does the editor serve?** Fiction writers? Nonfiction writers? Technical writers? I serve primarily coaches, entrepreneurs, and non-fiction writers who want to publish their Signature Book to gain visibility and credibility for their business.

2. **What kind of editing do you do?** Before you hire an editor, know what you want from them. Do you want copyediting to address grammar, punctuation, spelling, etc.? I do this. Do you want structural or technical editing that focuses on language issues, smoothing transitions, organizing content, flagging for fact checking, restructuring sentences and paragraphs to be clear and concise? I do this. Do you want deep developmental editing, someone to walk with you from beginning to end as you write, to address plotting, pacing, and literary or stylistic elements? I offer guidance to create a detailed outline for how-to and self-help content, but not for fiction. Do you want simple proofreading in the last stage before going to press? I do this.

3. **What genre does the editor most enjoy editing?** You will receive higher quality service from someone who enjoys your topic or genre than from someone who is bored by it. I especially enjoy how-to, self-help, and inspirational work. In

my own process of self-development I have nearly cleared the Barnes & Noble self-help shelves, read the books, done the exercises, and reaped steep rewards. I have a clear understanding of what works, both in the process and in the presentation. When my clients are published, their instructional books become trusted resources for me to refer to others.

4. **What is the editor's strong suit?** As an editor, I excel at streamlining sluggish text into words that are clear, concise, and compelling. As a coach, I open writers to a broader perspective, and I help self-proclaimed "non-writers" move past the doubt that keeps them from writing. I help my clients clarify their reason for writing and the focus of their content. I offer tools, techniques, and resources to better express the author's genius, to add value for readers, to invoke the voice of the heart, and to pique interest and response to enhance my client's business.

5. **What is the editor's guiding principle, and how does it show up in his or her work?** A go-to principle can keep an editor from getting mired in arduous details. My guiding principle is: Say it simply. I was once asked to edit a 10-page affidavit to be submitted in a divorce/child custody case. I streamlined sentences, sifted out irrelevant content, and condensed the length to under five

pages, adhering to court requirements without sacrificing critical content, thus saving time and money for the court, for counsel, and for the parties.

6. **What do the editor's clients have to say?** Testimonials tell you what the editor cannot. One of my clients, a seasoned middle-school teacher writing a guidebook for teachers, said: *I love how you make it more clear without changing my voice.* An engineer turned fiction writer in Houston, Texas, said to me:

> *Revising the opening paragraph was brilliant. Of the 8 or 9 other editors who have reviewed this work* **you are the first** *to suggest such a change. I am blown away by the profound impact of moving a single paragraph. So simple, yet it makes all the difference. Absolutely brilliant!*

7. **How does the editor charge?** You want to know this up front! Some choices include

- Hourly
- Per job
- By word count
- By page count
  Unless otherwise agreed between me and the author, my fee is based on word count of the manuscript in the form delivered by the author.

8. **Do you have rapport with the editor?** A good author-editor relationship starts with rapport. The best way to know if you are a harmonious fit is to engage in a live (not electronic) conversation. I offer an introductory strategy session to get acquainted, to discuss your needs, and to determine if we are a fit.

Editing is not just about fixing the grammar,
it's about fixing the clarity for your reader.
Ann Handley

You are brilliant, an expert in your field. You know your product and the topnotch quality of your service. If your reader has to slog through muddy material to decipher your message, chances are she will scratch her head in confusion and wander away. When that happens, she feels deflated, your business is stuck, and you continue to desperately seek new clients.

When people grasp your message, they know right off the bat whether they want what you offer. No muddle, no mess. You save them time and get them into action employing your wisdom for their benefit as well as your own.

A good editor can transform your presentation from ho-hum to zowie. Content that is crystal clear and succinct lights up a path to your door and compels your reader to engage with you. Your business is energized, and so are you. A good editor will energize your message, your business, and your happiness.

Nothing drags down writing more than
spreading good ideas over too many words.
Gregory Ciotti

To see if you and Nina have rapport,
visit www.NinaDurfee.com
and schedule a strategy session.

ABOUT THE AUTHOR

I am 4 years old, lying on my belly on the living room floor, when Mom brings me an end-of-the-day surprise—a Big Chief tablet and a fat yellow pencil. The lightweight cardstock cover is red with a rendering of the head of an American Indian in full headdress regalia. I flip back the cover to reveal the first page of flimsy newsprint in an off-white cast ruled with thin, pale blue lines. In that moment I know that I can create anything I want!

At the age of 4, Nina didn't know what that was, but she knew she was happier precisely carving out letters of the alphabet than she was trying to render an artistic image. In fourth grade she delighted in playing Scrabble, winning spelling bees, and diagraming sentences.

Clearly, words—not images—were her passion!

To this day, nothing gives her quite the thrill of a fresh, blank page and a pen full of ink.

Nina Durfee writes, coaches, edits, and gardens (in fair weather) from her home in the Rocky Mountains.

Printed in the United States
By Bookmasters